We Work Together
Learning about Teamwork

BY ALYSSA KREKELBERG

Published by The Child's World®
1980 Lookout Drive • Mankato, MN 56003-1705
800-599-READ • www.childsworld.com

Photographs ©: Ryan J. Lane/iStockphoto,
cover, 1, 5, 6, 9; iStockphoto, 10, 13, 14; Wave
Break Media/Shutterstock Images, 17, 18, 21

ISBN 9781503844551 (Reinforced Library Binding)
ISBN 9781503846715 (Portable Document Format)
ISBN 9781503847903 (Online Multi-user eBook)
LCCN 2019956646

Printed in the United States of America

ABOUT THE AUTHOR

Alyssa Krekelberg is a
children's book editor
and author. She lives
in Minnesota with her
hyper husky.

Contents

CHAPTER ONE

Working as a Team

Marshall, Cameron, and Dustin want to make a cake for their mom's birthday. Dustin asks their dad for help.

Their dad finds a recipe. "You will need to work together," he says. "I can help, too."

Sometimes you may need an adult to help you in the kitchen.

Following a recipe is important.

Before Dustin can read the list of ingredients, Cameron cracks an egg into the bowl. This makes Dustin mad. He wants to scream.

Instead, Dustin takes a deep breath and counts to five. When he is done, he does not want to scream anymore. He wants to work together.

"Let's do the steps in order," Dustin says. "That way the cake will bake correctly."

They boys listen to each other. They measure ingredients. Because they are working together, they know the cake will taste delicious.

You can do many things when you work together with others!

Some players do not want to work with their teammates. That can hurt the whole team.

10

CHAPTER TWO

Playing a Sport

Tara is on a basketball team. She dribbles the ball. She wants to score.

Then, a player from the other team moves in front of her. "Pass it to me!" her teammate Kevin says.

Tara does not want to pass the ball. She throws the ball at the hoop. But the other player knocks the ball away.

After the game, the coach talks to the team. "Make sure to work as a team," she says. "Every person has an important role."

Tara thinks about how she did not pass the ball. Kevin could have scored. By working together, they could have won the game.

It is important that people on a team work together.

13

Working together can solve many different types of problems.

During the next game, Tara dribbles the ball down the court. She smiles and passes the ball to Kevin. He throws the ball at the hoop, and the ball goes in!

Tara gives Kevin a high five. Because of their teamwork, their team wins the game.

CHAPTER THREE

A Team Project

Carlos is sad. He leans over his guitar. He starts to cry.

"What is wrong?" his teacher asks.

"We are supposed to practice, but Lauren and Mark will not play," Carlos says.

When people do not work together, it can make you sad or mad.

17

It is important to talk about your feelings with others.

"Why don't you tell your friends how you feel?" the teacher asks.

Carlos calls his friends over. "It makes me sad that we are not working together on this song," Carlos says. "I want to practice it."

Lauren and Mark smile. "Thank you for telling us how you feel," Lauren says. "We can start right now!"

The three friends stand close together. They look at the paper that tells them what to play.

Carlos counts to three. Then they start playing the song. It sounds great!

THINK ABOUT IT!

Can you think of a time when you needed to work as a team? What did you do to help your team do a great job?

What are three good things about teamwork?

It is fun to work together!

GLOSSARY

dribbles (DRIHB-els) Someone dribbles something when he or she bounces it up and down on the floor. The player dribbles the basketball down the court.

ingredients (in-GREE-dee-ints) Ingredients are things that are used to make food. The brothers read a list of ingredients.

measure (MEH-zhur) To measure something is to see how much of it you have. The brothers measure ingredients for the cake.

practice (PRAK-tiss) To practice is to work on something to make it better. Carlos wants to practice a song.

recipe (REH-sih-pee) A recipe is a list of materials and instructions to make food. The brothers looked at a recipe to make the birthday cake.

TO LEARN MORE

Books

Beard, Darleen Bailey. *Rosie Ross, Recess Boss: A Story about Problem Solving.* Vero Beach, FL: Rourke Educational Media, 2020.

Dinmont, Kerry. *Sad.* Mankato, MN: The Child's World, 2019.

Stark, Kristy. *The Best You: Win or Lose.* Huntington Beach, CA: Teacher Created Materials, 2018.

Websites

Visit our website for links about teamwork:
childsworld.com/links

Note to Parents, Teachers, and Librarians: We routinely verify our Web links to make sure they are safe and active sites. So encourage your readers to check them out!

INDEX